Merry Christmas
Brian Kinder

Buck and Ollie

A Christmas Time Story

Written and Illustrated by Brian Kinder

Copyright © 2019 by Brian Kinder

All rights reserved. This book, or parts thereof may not be reproduced in any form without permission.

Published by Kindersongs Publishing

PO Box 165051 Little Rock AR. 72216

www.kindersongs.com

CONTENTS

1. The Birch Bark Public Notice   1

2. Big Apple Tree   8

3. Winter Surprise   16

4. Beyond the Tall Pine Forest.   24

5. The Tree   34

6. The Journey Home   41

7. The Feast   52

8. The Gift   60

Chapter 1

The Birch Bark Public Notice

It was a crisp December morning on Hickory Mountain, and a small gray squirrel named Buck was busy filling his pockets with hickories he'd found among the fallen leaves. Suddenly he paused and sniffed the air. "It's going to snow," he thought, smiling to himself. Then with a laugh, he darted through the leaves back to his old, oak tree home where he deposited the nuts. Just then, something caught his attention. Several of the other forest residents were gathering not many yards away and gazing up at a tree where Woodpecker was busy pecking in a tack to hold a birch bark public notice.

Most everyone was present. There was Mrs. Rabbit and Mrs. Mole, in their familiar woolen shawls and mittens, and just like a pair of mittens, these ladies were almost always seen together. Yet unlike mittens they were a mismatch in size, Mrs. Rabbit, with her proud ears, being much the taller.

Joining the ladies now was the enormous Mr. Bear. He was truly immense and looking even larger this morning in his great hooded parka. Mrs. Rabbit and Mrs. Mole, if counted together, would still seem ever so slight in comparison.

O'Possum was also there, Irish as ever, sporting his best tweed and beret. And of course, there was Woodpecker.

They were all talking with one another now and laughing and shaking their heads up and down and making all manner of gestures so as to lend dimension to whatever it was they were talking about.

Buck straightened his bowtie, then pulling a shiny golden pocket watch from his vest, he checked the time. It was odd, he thought, especially for Mr. Bear to be up so early. He let his watch close with a snap, and in the same motion slipped it back into his vest. Brushing his clothing free of any remnants of the morning food gathering expedition, he left his chores to greet his friends.

"Good morning," Buck said in his most cheerful voice as he scampered through the leaves to where they were. No one answered nor even acknowledged his presence. Instead, they continued all the more in their frenzied conversing. Hoping they just hadn't heard him, he said, "Excuse me," and as if asking permission to speak, waved his paw to catch someone's attention. "Excuse me, please, but what's all the excitement about?"

O'Possum broke away from the conversation just long enough to answer. With his usual big grin and Irish brogue, he pointed to the tree and asked, "Have you not seen the public notice, lad?" With that O'Possum jumped back into the buzz of words and gestures, leaving Buck to focus on the birch bark.

"WINTER FEAST" was written in large letters at the top with smaller letters below. Just then, from a hole immediately above the notice, there popped a small furry head with whiskers and sleepy eyes. It was Ollie, the only other gray squirrel in the forest and Buck's best friend. He was still in his flannel gown and night cap.

"Ollie," cried Buck, "wake up! I've got terrific news!"

"I'm awake," yawned Ollie, trying to shield his face from the bright morning light. "How could anyone still be asleep with Woodpecker's pounding and all this jabbering going on? It sounds like half the forest is outside my door."

Ollie opened his eyes, blinked a few times, and surveying the source of all the chatter, exclaimed, "Oh my, did I say half the forest? It appears to be just about everyone." In a grander, more eloquent shade of oratory, Ollie, who was always one for speeches, spoke out to address the crowd below. "Good morning my friends, and to what do I owe the pleasure of this visit?" Not noticing no one had paid him any notice, Ollie continued. "I'd invite you in, but I'm afraid it would be dreadfully cramped."

"Ollie," interrupted Buck, "we're here because of the good news Woodpecker just left tacked to your tree."

"What good news?" asked Ollie.

"The Winter Feast, of course. See, it's on the notice just below you."

Ollie leaned out from his den opening to inspect the birch bark and Buck climbed up to meet him. "I'll read it," suggested

Buck, "since it's upside down for you." And quickly clearing his throat, he began.

"Winter Feast

Your presence is requested at

The annual Winter Feast

to be held on the next full moon

at the southern maple grove."

Buck finished the last few words almost shouting. And indeed, before he could finish, and without taking the time to put on so much as his slippers or coat, Ollie had climbed out to read the good news for himself. He looked at Buck and shouted, "The Winter Feast!"

There's hardly a tree big enough for two excited gray squirrels to express the kind of joy Buck and Ollie felt at that moment. They jumped, ran, scampered and chased each other all over the tree until, huffing and puffing, they stopped to catch their breath on a lower limb.

"Oh boy!" exclaimed Ollie, his tail still shaking from the excitement. "The Winter Feast! Can it be true? Here it is, time again for the Winter Feast, on the very next full moon. I can hardly wait." He cocked his head upward and a little to the side. "Hey, that's tomorrow evening." Then with a laugh he added, "I can still hardly wait! Oh, boy! The Winter Feast, the food, the games, the singing, the bonfire, the food. It's going to be great!"

From below, an ovation of laughter brought the two squirrels to their senses. In a flash, Buck and Ollie were down the tree and greeting their friends.

With paws together on his chest, Ollie spoke. "It's so good of you to invite us to the feast."

"It's good to have you two lively souls," replied Mr. Bear in his usual deep lazy voice. "It wouldn't be the same without you."

"It's just as much your feast as anyone's," squeaked Mrs. Mole, her eyes disappearing as she smiled.

"The Winter Feast is for everyone, both great and small," said Mrs. Rabbit.

"And who knows," added Woodpecker with a slightly scoffing chuckle, "perhaps even wise Mr. Owl will grace our forest with an appearance this year."

"Oh!" everyone exclaimed, as they thought, with nervous delight, of what they might wear, or how they might act if indeed Mr. Owl came to the feast. Most had never met Mr. Owl but they had all heard stories concerning his great wisdom and power. If only half of those stories were true, then he was surely someone to whom great respect and awe was to be given.

"Well, I'll be dressing up in my best," said O'Possum. Then turning to Mrs. Rabbit and Mrs. Mole, he added, "But it will be for the honor of our two lovely ladies here."

Long since widowed, both Mrs. Rabbit and Mrs. Mole often got quite a hoot from O'Possum's kidding and outrageous flattery, and this instance was no exception.

"O'Possum, you are so filled up with, I believe you call it, 'The blarney'," chuckled Mrs. Rabbit, and everyone concurred with a laugh. Then turning to Woodpecker, she said, "You'd better get that accordion of yours tuned up, Woodpecker. Mrs. Mole and I are coming to the Winter Feast with our dance cards filled."

"Hurrah!" came everyone's lighthearted response.

Then Mrs. Mole asked, "Do you really think wise Mr. Owl might come this year?"

"Not likely," said O'Possum. "I'd think it rare indeed for such nobility and caliber to be mingling with the common folk, such as we are."

"Well," said Mrs. Rabbit, "I'll be preparing my best recipe, and if he misses out, he'll just miss out."

"Carrot cake?" asked Ollie, "your world-famous carrot cake?"

"Well," said Mrs. Rabbit with a modest laugh. "I'm not sure 'World Famous' is how I would describe it, but yes, Ollie. I am planning to bake my carrot cake as well as some fresh nut bread." Her eyes sparkled. "That is, if you and Buck would be so kind as to gather some nuts for me."

"Of course, we will," replied Buck and Ollie.

With the mention of carrot cake, the other animals began describing again with great detail and gestures what savory dishes each would be bringing to share at the feast.

Ollie pulled Buck off to the side. "Buck," he whispered, "what about the gifts?"

"What gifts," asked Buck.

"For the feast," replied Ollie, motioning toward the birch bark. "The notice said our presents are requested. I just love presents; presents are wonderful fun! I love to give presents; I love to receive them, too!"

"Presents?" Buck thought aloud. "We didn't exchange gifts last year. Maybe I should ask."

"No, don't ask!" whispered Ollie. "I don't think it would be polite to ask about our presents."

"Oh, I see what you mean," Buck replied. "That wouldn't be proper, would it?" He looked a little embarrassed. "Thanks, Ollie"

"Don't mention it," Ollie said.

So, with arrangements well underway, all the forest animals each bid the other farewell as they went to their homes to begin their preparation for the annual Winter Feast

Chapter 2

Big Apple Tree

The rest of the morning, Buck and Ollie were busy gathering nuts. Not only did Mrs. Rabbit need walnuts for her carrot cake and fresh nut bread, but also hickories were needed for Woodpecker's savory rice and spice dish and his tasty berry surprise. Mrs. Mole's cheese and herb casserole called for lots of juicy chestnuts. And, of course, what would O'Possum's persimmon pie be without fresh pecans?

"Just think of all the food," shouted Buck from high up in their storehouse tree. He vanished into a dark hole and reappeared with yet another hickory from where they had been stored during the early autumn harvest. He tossed it down to Ollie who waited below.

Ollie's job was to secure the nuts in the sacks they had brought. He tried to position himself to catch the hickories, but the closest he came was when one hit him on the head.

"Mrs. Mole is brewing up some mint tea," Ollie hollered. "Can you smell it?"

"Yes, it reminds me of last year's feast," shouted Buck. "Mr. Bear's honey will sweeten it up fine. And Just think of Mrs.

Rabbit's fresh hot nut bread with butter and that same sweet honey."

"It's making me hungry now," groaned Ollie.

"No eating on the job," laughed Buck.

"That reminds me," Ollie said, with a mischievous giggle. "Mr. Bear offered to let us help him gather the honey crop again this year."

"That's a sweet job," said Buck. "Maybe later on, when we're not so busy."

"That's what I told him," chuckled Ollie. "I said, 'we'd love to help you Mr. Bear, but today we're busy doing nuttin'. Ha, ha, ha, ha, ha, ha, ha, ha, ha," Ollie laughed slapping his knees. "Get it Buck? Today we're busy doing nuttin. Ha, ha, ha, ha, ha."

Buck rolled his eyes, shook his head and released one last hickory. "Really Ollie, that joke was old when my Grandfather first heard it."

By the time Buck climbed down, Ollie had all the nuts in their proper bags. Together they delivered them to their respective destinations with Ollie checking names off a list he had made.

On the way back home, they began discussing what they should bring as gifts for their friends. Selecting a present for a forest animal is no easy task.

"Oh, Buck," said Ollie. "I have no idea what to give our friends at the feast."

"I can't think of anything either," replied Buck.

They each stopped to think. If you ever see squirrels just sitting motionlessly, they are probably thinking hard on something important.

"I've got it," Ollie suddenly exclaimed, "something everyone likes, fresh apples, red, crisp and juicy sweet."

"But Ollie," Buck said, "it's pretty late in the season..."

"There should be plenty at Big Apple Tree," Ollie said, and just like that, he was off and running.

Buck cried out, "Wait Ollie!" But Ollie didn't stop. Buck reluctantly gave chase to catch up with his hopeful grey companion.

'Big Apple Tree', as everyone referred to it, was broad at its base with large limbs extending upward and outward. Just how old the tree was, no one could say. It had been standing there twenty years earlier, though, when a young boy carved the name of his sweetheart into its bark, causing one of the great limbs to die, and eventually break off. A large cavity on the tree's upper trunk served as a reminder of those less fortunate days. Despite this, Big Apple Tree somehow always seemed full of life. It had long been a favorite rallying point for the forest residents, who were drawn to its springtime blossoms and summer time fruit. This, however, wasn't spring or summer, but rather late December.

Buck and Ollie arrived at the tree together, and Buck saw at a glance there were no apples to be found. Whether days or weeks late, it didn't matter. This year's bounty of ripe fruit had already been claimed.

Ollie seem bewildered as he gazed upward at the cold naked branches. He moved first here, then there, pausing each time to look again. But from no angle did he find any of the apples he most surely expected to see.

Buck quietly waited at the foot of another nearby tree. He could have said, 'I told you so,' but he didn't. He just stood there quietly as Ollie pitifully continued his search. After turning over several clumps of fallen leaves, Ollie, with his tail noticeably lowered, walked slowly over to Buck

"It's not easy giving gifts in the winter," Buck said, in an understanding kind of voice. "Everything's asleep till spring."

"I guess you're right," said Ollie. Then looking back at Big Apple Tree, he exclaimed loudly, "I wish you would have saved us some apples!"

Buck patted Ollie's shoulder to say, 'It was all right,' and they turned to go home. Just then they heard something they'd never heard before, a voice calling from Big Apple Tree.

"I'm sorry all the apples are gone."

Ollie started to say, 'That's okay,' but got only as far as "That's O...!" He looked at Buck, who was already looking at him, and together they turned around to look at Big Apple Tree. To their astonishment it spoke again.

"I didn't know squirrels were so fond of apples."

Buck, seeing Ollie still frozen with his mouth in an 'O' shape, began. "We wanted, that is, Ollie wanted to give some of your, uh, fine apples as gifts to our friends at the Winter Feast. I told Ollie it was a little late for apples, but I guess he had to see for himself. We wouldn't have bothered you, had it not been so important."

"Important?" asked the tree.

"Yes," said Buck, "The Winter Feast is tomorrow evening, and unless we can find a gift, I guess we won't be able to go."

"You would miss the Winter Feast?" asked the tree.

"I'm afraid we'd have to," said Buck. "You see, the birch bark public notice said our presents are requested."

"Your presents? Oh! Your presence!" chuckled the tree. "Yes, I believe I'm beginning to understand now."

With the tree's friendly chuckle, Buck began feeling much the more comfortable now. He continued his explanation as if it were the most natural thing in the world to be talking to a tree, and that he did this sort of thing all the time. "We wanted to surprise everyone with something special," he said, "but we can think of nothing".

"Well," said the tree. "it is a shame there are no apples." His voice was deep, and so kind. "Perhaps I could suggest a different gift for your friends."

Finding his voice, Ollie exclaimed, "A different gift?"

"Yes," replied the tree. "I know of another tree that could provide you with a different gift, a truly wonderful gift for you to surprise your friends. Might you be interested?"

Buck and Ollie could hardly believe their ears. "Yes, please tell us," they said.

"My pleasure," replied the tree. "If you travel east from these woods you will come to a tall pine forest. Are you familiar with it?"

Buck and Ollie nodded, and the tree continued.

"Just beyond the tall pine forest is a deep valley. There's only one tree to be found in this valley, and this will be the tree you are looking for. I'm sure you can find it."

"Sure, we can," exclaimed Ollie. "We've never ventured that far; never had a reason to. But we've seen the tall pine forest, and if the valley is just beyond it, I'm sure we can find the tree. We'll start out immediately."

Buck nudged Ollie and said, "Perhaps we should wait until tomorrow."

"Your friend is right," said the tree. "The sun will be setting soon. You can begin tomorrow morning and be back home by late afternoon."

"That's perfect!" exclaimed Ollie. "Just in time for the Winter Feast."

"Now, you'll need something to carry the gifts back home, perhaps a basket," suggested the tree.

"Oh of course," said Buck. Then after an awkward pause he added, "By the way, you haven't yet told us what the gift is."

"Well," replied the tree with a laugh, "that's to be a surprise. You did say the gift was to be a surprise, didn't you?"

Buck and Ollie looked at each other and then back to the tree. "Well, yes," said Ollie.

And Buck added, "A good surprise, that is."

"It will be a wonderful surprise and a wonderful gift," assured Big Apple Tree.

"Yes, I'm sure it will be," said Ollie, his eyes beaming. "How can we ever thank you enough?"

"Don't mention it," replied the tree.

With that, Buck and Ollie bid farewell to Big Apple Tree and started for home. "Wow!" said Ollie, "a talking tree. I didn't even know trees could talk. Does your tree ever talk to you, Buck?"

"Sometimes, when it's windy, it creaks a little," said Buck.

"Mine never talks to me," replied Ollie. "I didn't even see his mouth move. Did you Buck?"

"I'm not even sure I knew where his mouth was," replied Buck.

The sun was setting now, and one could hear Buck and Ollie still chattering as they arrived at their home woods. Actually, Ollie was doing most of the talking. He was trying to guess what they would find the next day just beyond the tall pine forest.

Chapter 3

Winter Surprise

Buck was awakened the next morning by the familiar sound of small feet running up the outside of his tree. It was Ollie, of course, and as Ollie reached the den opening and poked his head in, he called down, "Buck, Buck, are you awake?"

Buck thought to himself, 'Maybe if I just lay here and pretend to be asleep.'

Just then, from up above, he heard another familiar sound. It was the sound of a nut bounding downward inside his tree. Ollie listened, too, as the nut he had just dropped made its way down the den. Bing, bang, bong. "Ouch!" A light came on down inside the tree, and now Ollie could hear Buck's little feet making their way up to him.

"I knew it! I knew it!" exclaimed Buck as he reached the den opening.

"Good morning, Buck," said Ollie.

"Morning?" Buck shouted. He straightened himself and looked past Ollie into the darkness. "So, you call this morning?"

"Shhhhh," said Ollie, his eyes wide open, his mouth half covered with his paw. "You'll wake everyone."

"That's what I mean," replied Buck in a great fluster. "Everybody's asleep! Everybody should be sleep. It's still dark out."

After another round of shushing on Ollie's part, Buck quieted down a bit, though the irritation could still be heard in his voice. "I don't suppose I should be surprised," Buck said. "I've seen that look in your eyes before."

"What look in my eyes?" asked Ollie.

"That look," said Buck. "That same look you have when the forest flowers first bloom, or when the leaves first begin to change color, or when we get the first winter snow. Well you had that look on your face last night at Big Apple Tree, and I said to myself, 'Buck, I'd wager a bushel of beech nuts that Ollie will be waking you up first thing in the morning.' And I'd have won that bet too, because here you are."

"Oh Buck," said Ollie, "I am so lucky to have a friend like you who understands. Are you about ready to start out for the tall pine forest?"

"Ready?" Buck asked in disbelief. "I just woke up, I haven't had breakfast, and it's black as winter walnuts out there. No, I am not ready!"

"Good idea, Buck," said Ollie, "I haven't had my breakfast either. Let's eat first then start out."

"But not before light," insisted Buck. "I still can't believe you found my tree in this darkness."

"Oh, that was easy," said Ollie. "Last evening, just before dark, I tied a piece of string from my tree to yours, and this morning I simply followed it here."

"If it were morning," said Buck, "you wouldn't need a string to find my tree." With that he disappeared into his den and Ollie followed.

After a simple breakfast of toasted nut bread and marmalade, Buck leaned back to sip on a second cup of steaming hot tea. Ollie, anxious to leave, yet forced to wait out the dawn, occupied himself by pulling out a piece of paper from his coat pocket and looking it over. It was a list he had made the night before in preparation for the trip.

Buck knew it was like a hundred other lists he had seen Ollie make in the past, and Ollie followed his predictable approach by marking through items he had accomplished. He marked though the line that read, 'Wake Buck Up.' It seemed to give him a sense of achievement to see items marked off, and the bigger the list, the greater the accomplishment and satisfaction.

Ollie made his way up to the den opening to check on the sunrise. Returning with a sigh, he picked up his pencil and again looked over the list. On a new line he wrote, 'Eat Breakfast,' then quickly, and with a look of satisfaction, he drew a line through it.

Buck just shook his head, chuckled softly to himself and continued sipping his tea. Ollie folded his list, returning it to his coat pocket, then moments later, he again darted up to the den opening to check on the sunrise.

This was his ninth trip in fifteen minutes. On the previous trips, Buck knew it was still dark by Ollie's loud sighs upon reaching the den's opening. This time, however, Ollie ran back down and with great whispers exclaimed, "The sun is coming up! The sun is coming up! It's time to go Buck!"

Buck took one last sip of tea and followed Ollie who was already up the tree and out the hole. At the den opening, Buck looked out toward the east. The sun, trying to peek over the horizon, was persimmon red. The silhouettes of trees were spooky black patterns etched in the sky.

Buck, of course, thought it was still much too early, but he also realized Ollie, who had already climbed out and now waited below, wouldn't wait another minute. "Black as winter walnuts, Buck groaned."

Climbing down, he noticed Ollie had brought a large wicker basket as Big Apple Tree had suggested. The basket was twice the size of any squirrel, and Buck wondered if perhaps it wasn't too big. "Where on earth did you find this basket, Ollie?"

"Isn't it great, Buck?" whispered Ollie. "It washed up on the riverbank after a big summer rain. I was afraid when it dried it might shrink, but it didn't."

"Maybe I could borrow it," laughed Buck, "for the times when Mr. Bear comes to spend the night and needs a bed to sleep in." Buck began laughing, and then tried to hush up, but the best he could do was to make short snorting sounds as his whole body quaked.

"Oh, it's not that big," said Ollie, crossing his arms. "We can take turns carrying it, if that's okay with you." And then, to change the subject, he said, "I wonder what wonderful gifts it will hold on the way back."

"Who knows?" Buck grunted, as he picked up the basket, shuffling a little to balance it over his head. "I just hope it's not too heavy."

With that, they were off. If you or any other forest animal had been up, and indeed if it had been light enough to see, you would have seen Buck and Ollie sneaking through the woods toward the orange sunrise on their way to the tall pine forest.

Actually, Ollie was sneaking along from tree to tree while Buck stuck to the path and carried the basket.

Buck didn't want to be seen leaving the forest any more than Ollie, but Buck's reasons were different. Ollie worried about spoiling everyone's Winter Feast surprise, while Buck, on the other hand, didn't want anyone to think he was foolish enough to be out at that hour. As it was, they left unnoticed, in spite of all the leaves Ollie crunched as he snuck about.

They had walked only a little way beyond their own woods when Ollie suddenly stopped. With eyes and mouth wide open he turned to Buck and exclaimed, "it's snowing!"

Sure enough, the red sky had given way to grey clouds bringing the season's first snow. Buck dropped the basket with a loud, happy "HI HO!" Together the two furry companions jumped around a bit, pulling numerous squirrel capers to properly welcome the winter's first white offering.

Ollie had that wonderfully bewildered expression of delight all over his little squirrel face as he rolled around and tried to catch snowflakes on his tongue. It was falling quite hard now, and the dawn brought enough light to see the ground beginning to turn white.

Buck did not like to admit it, but he was just as excited as Ollie. The snow seemed to flood his mind with a thousand pleasant memories of winter days spent playing checkers with Ollie by the cozy fireplace. And how often the crackling of the fire was the only sound to be heard as he and Ollie contemplated which checker to move. He remembered how the food stored up during the fall tasted so much better with snow on the ground, and how hours upon carefree hours were spent simply watching the snow fall and enjoying the wonder of it all from the safety of his tree.

Buck's joyful reminiscing suddenly turned to thoughts of great concern as he realized he was not safely within his own tree. He wasn't even in his own woods, but rather on a journey to who knows where. He cried out, "Ollie!"

Buck's tone caused Ollie to stop and look up, and now Ollie could see by the expression on Buck's face that something was dreadfully wrong.

"Ollie," Buck said, firmly, "we can't go on."

"What do you mean, Buck?" asked Ollie.

"What I mean is, we can't go beyond the tall pine forest today. There's no way!" Buck insisted. "In fact we must return home immediately."

Chapter 4

Beyond the Tall Pine Forest

Ollie had been lying flat on his back, joyfully catching snowflakes on his tongue. Buck's words, however, quickly put an end to that.

Ollie looked at Buck in disbelief. "You're teasing me, aren't you Buck? We can't turn back now, we've hardly even begun."

"Oh, Ollie, I wish I were teasing," said Buck. "but it would be too dangerous. We simply cannot continue this journey, not in this snow. It's just fortunate we haven't gone any further, or otherwise we'd really be in a fix."

Ollie jumped up. "What do you mean, we'd be in a fix?"

Buck pointed toward the ground. "The path is already covering with snow, and it's just starting. It looks to me like this snowfall could last all day, or even longer. Why, for all we know, it may not stop 'til the whole world is a giant snowball."

"A giant snowball!" Ollie exclaimed, "Buck, you exaggerate more than all creatures in the world put together. You're not going to let this little snow scare you away from the greatest adventure of your life, are you?"

Buck thought he was using good sense in this matter, and he resented Ollie's suggestion that perhaps this cautious path he wanted to retreat upon was due to his lack of daring. "Ollie," he said, "I'm every bit as venturesome as you, but I'm just trying to be reasonable, and for the life of me, I don't understand why you won't be also." Then Buck matured his tone, not unlike that of a schoolmaster, and striking a scholarly pose said, "You know the old saying….

'Stay close to home, and do not roam

When snow is on the ground

The place to be is your own tree

Not somewhere wondering around'

It's easy enough, even in your own woods, to find yourself turned around when it snows, but if we try to go into a strange new forest, we'll never find our way back!"

"But Buck, we won't get lost," assured Ollie. "We can find our way there and back without any problem. Lost? No way! Besides, the snow will soon stop, and together we'll make it just fine."

"I don't know," said Buck, looking around. "It's snowing pretty hard."

"Everyone's counting on us, Buck," said Ollie, "and the sooner we get there, the sooner we'll get back."

This exchange went on and on with much additional persuasion on Ollie's part, met by considerably more foot dragging by Buck. Indeed, it might have resulted in a stalemate had it not been for Ollie suggesting that perhaps he might go on without Buck.

Buck was quite taken back by this thought. He knew if he allowed Ollie to go on alone, his friend would most likely wind up lost forever in a snowstorm, and Buck would never be able to forgive himself. On the other hand, if somehow Ollie returned triumphant with tales of adventure and untold treasure from a mysterious talking tree, his regret would also be boundless and enduring. Just which consequence seemed weightier did not matter, for Buck knew he was in a no-win situation. "Oh, all right then," he conceded. "We'll chance it together."

"That's the spirit, Buck," exclaimed Ollie! "The sooner we start, the sooner we'll be back."

"Or the sooner we get lost and not found 'til the spring thaw," groaned Buck.

Ollie insisted on carrying the basket now, and with Buck in the lead they continued toward the tall pine forest. The rustling of leaves soon gave way to the soft patting of small feet on fresh snow. They kept walking and the snow kept falling and the deeper it got the more Ollie found it increasingly difficult to manage the basket. He wasn't, however, even considering complaining or asking for help for fear that Buck would again insist on turning back.

They trudged onward toward their mysterious destination with Buck now serving as navigator. After some time, he stopped, and a few seconds later, when Ollie caught up, Buck suggested they rest for a while.

"If you think so," puffed Ollie, trying to catch his breath. Buck wasn't tired, but he had noticed how Ollie was having trouble carrying the basket in the deepening snow. Without mentioning the problem, they both sat quietly trying to think of a way to more easily transport the basket.

Ollie watched as the snowflakes fell softly downward. Except for his continued puffing, there was total silence.

Then suddenly Buck jumped up and exclaimed, "I've got it!" Quickly he ran over to a group of small hickory saplings, and after only a few moments of diligent tooth work, he returned, dragging a bundle of four or five switches.

Ollie had no idea what Buck was up to but felt sure his friend had somehow already solved the problem in his mind and that in no time at all, and before their very eyes, some sort of apparatus would magically appear to help transport the basket. "Come on, Buck," he shouted.

Buck worked deliberately, wasting no time. First, he stripped the bark from two of the long, thin hickory sticks. Then he cut and cut again. After a bit of bending and assembling, he used the tender hickory bark strips to tie the first section of his handiwork to the bottom of the basket.

Ollie suddenly realized what Buck was doing. "A sleigh," he exclaimed, "you're building a sleigh." Ollie perched himself upon the overturned basket and from there he happily watched as his friend worked. "Buck, you're the greatest!" he cheered.

As Buck finished the second runner, and was securing it to the sleigh, Ollie jumped down and together they turned the basket right side up. Though not fancy in any sense of the word, it was indeed a sleigh with two curved hickory runners supporting the basket. Buck knotted a long strip of hickory bark rope to the front, and as he pulled, Ollie pushed from behind. The sleigh-basket glided across the snow with such wonderful ease they couldn't help shouting for joy.

Together they pushed and pulled the sleigh-basket up the hills, then laughing and singing they would jump inside and ride down. Filled with new hope and energy, they made great time.

"I'm glad for the snow," said Ollie. "It hasn't hurt us; it's helped us."

"I guess you're right," said Buck. "If I've figured it correctly, the tall pine forest should be just over the next hill."

"Great," said Ollie. But as they slid down the next hill, there was no tall pine forest. It wasn't to be found over the next hill either. After another hill and still no tall pine forest, even Ollie was beginning to worry.

Buck said they never should have left their own woodlands and perhaps they should return before the snow covered their tracks completely. Ollie was beginning to have the same thoughts, but somehow suggested trying just one more hill. Unfortunately, it also led nowhere, and now both Buck and Ollie were as discouraged as two grey squirrels could be.

Ollie sighed "I guess you're right, Buck. Maybe we should go back."

Sadly, they turned the sleigh-basket around, and with less energy and no singing, they began their ascent back up the slope, following in their own tracks. As they crested the hill and were climbing in to ride down the other side, Ollie asked if he could steer. Buck didn't really trust Ollie's sledding abilities, but seeing the look of gloom on his companion's face, he couldn't say no. "Just lean the way you want to turn, and stay with our tracks," instructed Buck.

"I know," said Ollie. And off they went.

Right from the start of Ollie's first ever run, Buck felt the sleigh was traveling faster than before, but dismissed these feelings to his being the passenger now, and not the pilot. Suddenly, though, he realized it was not his imagination. The hill was indeed becoming longer and much steeper than he had first thought. They were traveling quite rapidly now, and you can imagine Buck's uneasiness when Ollie turned around and said, "Thanks Buck, for letting me steer."

"Watch where you're going!" shrieked Buck.

The trail Ollie was to follow went left, but somehow the sleigh went right. To their horror, and with no time to even blink, they were sailing down the steepest grade imaginable. Faster and faster they flew just missing tree after menacing tree, that seemed to leap out from nowhere to block their path.

"We're out of control," shouted Buck!

"Hold on!" cried Ollie.

Together they clung to each other at the bottom of the sleigh-basket, gritting their teeth and preparing as best they could for a great crash, but it never came. Instead, the sleigh-basket slowed and finally stopped.

Still shaking with fear, Buck and Ollie slowly pulled themselves up from the bottom of the basket and looked around.

"Ollie," said Buck. "Do you see where we are?"

To their astonishment, they were in the middle of the tall pine forest. Ollie's wrong turn somehow turned out right after all.

"Ollie, you are wonderful," shouted Buck and he gave him a big hug.

"Ah, it was nothing, probably just luck," replied Ollie.

They climbed out of the sleigh and after determining their location, and recalculating directions, they started off again through the tall pines. The sleigh once again moved with ease as the two grey squirrels resumed their happy songs. After a while, though, the way grew steeper and steeper. Neither squirrel mentioned it, but rather labored all the more. Finally, Buck said, "It sure will be easier coming back this way."

Ollie chuckled and said, "I bet you'll want to steer then."

Together they paused a moment to laugh and rest. Ollie lay back in the snow, trying again to catch the falling flakes in his mouth. Buck looked up the hill and exclaimed, "There's the end of the tall pine forest, just ahead!"

Ollie jumped to his feet and looked up the hill to where his friend was pointing. It was just as Buck had said. The eastern boundary of the tall pine forest was only a short distance away. Again, Buck and Ollie took their positions at the sleigh and started up the hill. The ground began leveling out as they reached the summit and forest's edge.

"The tree we're looking for must be there," puffed Ollie as he pointed down the other side of the hill.

"There it is!" shouted Buck.

Sure enough, in the valley below stood a tall dark shadow contrasted against the falling snow. Buck and Ollie knew it was a tree, the only tree around. And though, because of the falling snow, they couldn't tell what kind of tree it was, their excitement grew as they realized the wonderful surprise promised by Big Apple Tree waited just below.

Chapter 5

The Tree

Ollie climbed into the basket and positioned himself to steer. "Come on, Buck."

Buck gave the sleigh a push to start it on its way then jumped in. "Steer for the tree," he said.

"I wonder what kind of tree it is?" said Ollie.

"And what treasures it will hold?" wondered Buck. He began to envision gold and silver, diamonds, rubies and other precious gems. "Perhaps," he thought, "the tree would grant wishes, or have secret powers."

All these thoughts were running through his mind, but then Ollie shouted, "It looks like a pine tree."

"A what?" yelled Buck, refusing to believe his ears. He strained his eyes, blinking several times to clear his vision from the steady onslaught of snowflakes hitting his face. "It must just look like a pine tree," he said. He was about to continue, but suddenly realized the sleigh was once again going much too fast and this time heading directly for the tree. "Watch where you're going!" he shouted, but it was too late. With a tremendous bang the sleigh-basket collided squarely with the tree. The two grey squirrels had just enough time to brace themselves before impact.

Ollie was right. It was a pine tree, and their violent meeting was such that it jarred loose several pinecones, which fell to the snow all around its base. Buck and Ollie lay in a furry heap at the bottom of the basket.

"Are you okay?" whispered Ollie.

"My head's a little sore," groaned Buck, "but I guess I'm fine."

"I can't feel my tail," Ollie said with a worried voice.

"That's my tail, Ollie," said Buck.

"Oh, sorry," Ollie said, with a laugh. "We really need to get some brakes on the sleigh-basket Buck."

"Why?" Buck asked, rolling his eyes. "All you have to do is slam us into the nearest tree and it stops us real fast?"

"Well you told me to steer for the tree," said Ollie.

"And you did a bang-up job of that," replied Buck, rubbing his head.

Helping each other up and out of the sleigh-basket, they began surveying the tree and their situation.

"This can't be right," said Buck. "This is just a regular old pine tree. We have a whole forest of them back home."

"But this is the valley beyond the tall pine forest, and this is the only tree around; it must be the right one," said Ollie.

"No, Ollie," Buck said, "The tree we're looking for has wonderful presents to surprise our friends at the Winter Feast, remember? If this is the right tree, where are the presents?"

Just then, from up above, something fell, and as luck would have it, bounced off Buck's already sore head and landed in the sleigh-basket. Buck was again rubbing his head and looking at Ollie as if Ollie were somehow to blame.

"Honest, Buck," said Ollie with his paw raised, "I didn't do it. Whatever it was, it's in the basket." Cautiously, they peered over the basket's edge, and there they saw a single snow-covered pinecone.

"That's it!" shouted Ollie, pointing to the pinecone.

"What's it?" asked Buck.

"Don't you see, Buck?" said Ollie. "We're to give a snow-covered pinecone to each of our friends at the Winter Feast."

Buck stepped back and looked at Ollie in disbelief. "Are you crazy?" he said. "What would our friends want with a silly old pinecone? And even if they wanted a pinecone, which I seriously doubt, there are pinecones all over our forest."

"But these pinecones are different, special," Ollie said, "and one just jumped in the sleigh basket to show us. What a surprise! Remember, Big Apple Tree told us it would be a surprise. This must be the tree, it's the only tree around. And the pinecones must be what we're to give our friends, they're all the tree has to offer. Oh, I'm sure this is what we came for!" exclaimed Ollie, all out of breath.

Buck gave out a groan. "Talking trees and jumping pinecones!" Rolling his eyes and looking upward, he wondered now if Ollie hadn't shaken loose a few marbles when they collided with the tree. His thoughts were interrupted as a single ray of sunshine broke through the clouds and fell directly on him and Ollie.

Together they looked upward as patches of blue sky began to appear. The last of the snowflakes were falling now, catching the sun's light, and returning it again like a shower of diamonds slowly and softly descending from the heavens.

"It's stopped snowing, Buck," said Ollie.

The whole valley suddenly became a brilliant glow of illumination until it hurt their eyes. The sunlight made everything so much brighter and more beautiful. Buck looked around. He could see the whole valley now and indeed the pine tree they had collided with was the only tree to be seen.

Ollie picked up a pinecone and said, "I don't understand it all, Buck, but I just somehow know this is what Big Apple Tree intended for us to give to our forest friends. Will you help me, or do you think I'm crazy?"

Buck laughed one of those 'I give up' kind of laughs. Shaking his head, he said, "Here's what I think. I think we both must be crazy to be out here in the first place. Here we are in the middle of nowhere because a tree, a tree mind you, tells us that this tree would provide us a wonderful surprise to give our friends at the Winter Feast. Well, I must say this is a surprise. In fact, pinecones were somehow the last things I thought we'd be giving as presents."

After a wry chuckle, Buck continued, "The adventure of a lifetime," he said, trying as much as possible to make it sound as Ollie had. He looked down at his feet, then at the tree, then once again at the sky.

"I suppose," He said, "it just stands to reason that if I'm crazy enough to have come this far, not to mention in a snow storm, then I'm probably crazy enough to see this adventure through. Sure, Ollie, I'll help. Besides, we have to go home anyway. We may as well take these pinecones with us."

"Buck, you're the best friend a squirrel could ever have," cheered Ollie, as he tossed his pinecone in the basket.

Together they went to work and in a short time had picked up all the fallen pinecones. There was still one, however, on a tiny upper limb of the tree. Ollie offered to retrieve it, but Buck said they had just enough by his count.

Now ready to leave, Buck turned and addressed the tree. "I don't suppose you would tell us what we're to do with all these pinecones would you, Pine Tree?" He and Ollie waited to hear if the pine tree would answer. There was only silence.

"I guess he's not a big talker like Big Apple Tree," whispered Ollie. Then addressing the tree, himself, Ollie said, "Thank you for the pinecones." Still there was no reply.

Buck broke the silence. "Push or pull Ollie," he asked?

This time Ollie elected to pull the sleigh, but first he had to again take his list from his pocket and scratch through a few more lines with the pencil.

"And what did you mark through this time?" asked Buck.

"Find the tree, and get the presents," answered Ollie, with a look of satisfaction.

So, Buck and Ollie started off for home, their sleigh-basket filled with the snow-covered pinecones they planned to give as gifts to their friends later that evening at the Winter Feast.

Chapter 6

The Journey Home

It would be much easier for Buck and Ollie to find their way home, now that it had stopped snowing. Their morning journey had left a trail which, when followed in reverse, would simply bring them back to their own forest. The sleigh-basket, now filled with pinecones, was not as easily pushed and pulled as before, but Buck and Ollie could still ride it down hills. And comforted with the fact they were finally heading home, their trip continued with much joy and singing. They sang:

'Twice the joy and half the sorrows

When you share them with a friend

Friends today and friends tomorrow

True friendship will never end.'

"I'm starving," said Ollie, presently. "I don't suppose you packed anything to eat in one of your pockets there, did you Buck?"

"Not so much as an acorn," said Buck, and with a chuckle he added, "and I just bet you're going to tell me now that on the list you made, with such important items as 'Wake up,' 'Shut off alarm clock,' and 'Get dressed,' you didn't think to write down, 'Pack a lunch,' so as not to perish in the wilderness."

"Oh Buck," said Ollie, in his own defense. "You know good and well that we both were planning to eat what we found here and there on the ground while we traveled, and we would have, too, except for the snow on the ground."

"What's the matter, Ollie," laughed Buck, "are you tired of eating snowflakes?"

"I've always heard each snowflake is different," Ollie said, "but these all taste the same to me."

"Just think, Ollie," Buck said, in overdramatic tones, "right under our feet, at this very moment, just below the snow are nuts of every size and variety: crisp juicy hickory nuts, plump ripe pecans, mouthwatering walnuts."

"Stop it, Buck, you're making me even more hungry!" cried Ollie, with a laugh. Then he added, "But just think of all the food at the feast tonight: tasty cheese casserole, succulent berry surprise, scrumptious…" He was about to continue, but Buck, beaten at his own game, was now the one asking for mercy.

Changing the subject, Ollie asked, "Buck, do you think Mr. Owl will come to the feast tonight?"

"I hope so," said Buck. "I've heard a lot about him, and I've always wanted to meet him."

"Me too," said Ollie, "but I think I want to meet him in the same peculiar way I'd like to someday see a tornado."

"I know what you mean," replied Buck. "Just to think of seeing him face to face sort of scares me, but I'd gladly be scared for the chance."

Ollie looked around as if worried someone could be listening in, and then in a low voice said, "Woodpecker acted like meeting Mr. Owl was nothing special. He said Mr. Owl was just another bird to him."

"Well," said Buck, "Woodpecker has hammered his head against so many trees, he probably doesn't have enough sense to be scared." With that, Buck and Ollie shared one of their better laughs of the day.

They traveled all afternoon, and the sun, peering in and out of the fluffy clouds, went from bright yellow to orange as it slowly edged toward the horizon. They had just finished one of their many squirrel choruses when Ollie asked, "How much further, Buck?"

"Not far," replied Buck, but he didn't sound as excited as you might expect. Each step he and Ollie took brought them closer to their home woods, and as comforting as this thought should have been, Buck was becoming increasingly more ill at ease as each step also found the trail becoming more and more difficult to follow. "The snow that fell after we passed this way has all but covered our tracks," he said.

"Then we must be close to home, right Buck?" asked Ollie.

"Just a few more hills, I suppose," said Buck. "That is if we don't get lost."

"Lost!" exclaimed Ollie, "Well I hope we don't get lost."

"Oh," said Buck, sounding a bit perturbed, "so now it's, 'I hope we don't get lost', is it? This morning you were saying we could never get lost."

"Well, we're not lost yet," said Ollie.

Buck was about to answer, but just then the faint trail by which he was navigating suddenly ended. He stopped in his tracks then bent down to the ground for a closer look.

Ollie, who was pushing from the rear of the sleigh, and quite unaware his friend had stopped, continued forward and accidentally banged right into Buck with the sleigh-basket. Buck got a face full of snow, and Ollie had to help him up while trying not to laugh in the process.

A stern lecture about watching the trail is what Ollie expected, but Buck had more important matters at hand. "Ollie," he said, "we've just run out of trail to follow."

Ollie said nothing, but rather looked to his friend to continue. Buck turned and looked on up ahead to where the trail would have been. After what seemed to Ollie an awfully long time, Buck pointed and said, "Do you see that tallest cedar tree way over on the hill?"

"Is that our forest home?" asked Ollie, hardly even looking where Buck was pointing.

"No," said Buck, "but before this trail ended, we had been traveling on a pretty much straight course. If we continue in that same direction, it would take us toward that cedar. I think that unless we have a reason to change direction, we should just continue straight ahead."

"Well," said Ollie, impatiently, "let's go, then."

They started off once again, but this time with a much more rapid and urgent pace. Buck pulled, keeping his eyes all the while on the large cedar. Ollie pushed and looked all about the woods.

Suddenly Ollie cried, "Stop, Buck!" The sleigh came to a halt and now Ollie was looking and pointing off in a totally different direction. "See that hickory tree over there, Buck? Isn't that our favorite store house hickory?"

Ollie was convinced, and even ready to turn the sleigh-basket in this new direction, but Buck said, "Wait a minute." He studied the tree for a moment and though it bore some resemblance to the hickory of which Ollie referred, reason told him this could not be the same tree. "Ollie, that can't be our hickory. Our hickory is to the west of our home woods, nowhere around here."

Ollie looked so confused that Buck couldn't help feeling sorry for him. "Come on, Ollie," he said, let's stay on this course. I'm sure we'll find our way home soon."

Reluctantly, Ollie agreed, and together they started again toward the cedar. Twice more Ollie saw trees which he was sure had come from their home woods, and either of these would have easily lured him away from their course had it not been for Buck's persistence. As it was, they stuck to Buck's plan, and it was a good thing they did, for upon reaching the large cedar, they discovered the stand of hickory saplings from which Buck had fashioned the runners for the sleigh.

"We're not lost!" Buck shouted, pointing to the saplings. "We're almost home!"

"I told you we couldn't get lost," cheered Ollie. "How much further, Buck?"

"Our home is just over the next hill," replied Buck, "and from the looks of the sun, we're not a minute too soon."

"Right, Buck," replied Ollie. "We'll spruce up a little then start out again for the southern maple grove."

Buck suddenly stopped. "Ollie," he cried, "I forgot the Winter Feast is at the southern maple grove. I had it in my mind that over the next hill we'd see a bonfire and smell the good food."

"Don't worry, Buck," said Ollie, "the southern maple grove is just a short distance from where we live."

"A short distance by daylight, but we'll soon be without daylight," said Buck. "Maybe O'Possum can see at night, but we can't. How will we travel in the dark?"

"If we hurry," said Ollie, "we can probably make it before dark."

Buck and Ollie topped the hill, and sure enough there was their own forest. It was so good to be home. Together they stopped the sleigh-basket and ran to their own trees to smarten up a bit before leaving for the party. As Buck reached his home, he found a note, which he read as he dressed. It was from Mrs. Rabbit, and said,

'Dear Buck and Ollie,

We've all gone to the Southern Maple Grove.

Please join us for the Winter Feast.

Sincerely,

Mrs. Rabbit

P.S. Isn't the snow lovely?'

Buck changed ties, and in no time was ready. And yet in that time the sun had slipped away and only twilight remained.

Ollie returned just as quickly, his fur brushed and smelling of his best cologne. With him, he carried a candle.

"Good thinking, Ollie," said Buck.

Ollie looked around and said, "I guess everyone's already left."

"You're right," said Buck, telling him about Mrs. Rabbit's note.

"I was hoping we could all go together," said Ollie, "but at least you and I will be able to follow in their footprints."

"That's right," exclaimed Buck, for he was wondering how he and Ollie would find their way.

Again, they set the sleigh-basket in motion, following their friend's footprints toward the southern maple grove. They were making great time, but soon the twilight ended, and only darkness remained. The trail became impossible to follow.

"Come on, Ollie, it's this way," said Buck.

"No, I think it's this other way," replied Ollie.

Together they stopped and looked at each other. It was so dark that even at that closeness they appeared only as black shapes to each other.

"Time for the candle, Ollie," said Buck. "I'm glad you thought to bring it."

"I remembered to bring a match, too," Ollie said, proudly.

He reached into his coat pocket and retrieved the candle along with a single wooden kitchen match. Buck said nothing yet wondered why Ollie couldn't just as easily have brought along a whole box of matches. Ollie handed the candle to Buck, and immediately began attempting to light the match by striking it on the inner zipper of his coat. Buck, sensing there would be no second chance, quickly cupped his little paws around the candle, protecting it from any breezes that might blow it out.

Zip, zip, zip came the sound of the match against Ollie's zipper and yet the match did not light. Buck was about to suggest letting him try, but then, on Ollie's next try, there was a soft pop and a sizzling flame. The match burned bright, as bright as Buck and Ollie's hopes, but just as quickly, the bright flame simply went out leaving them in darkness.

"Oh no!" groaned Buck in great despair as he stood there holding the now useless candle.

"I'm sorry Buck," whispered Ollie. "I should have brought more matches. Now what are we going to do?"

Buck did his best not to sound worried as he tried to assure Ollie that everything would somehow be okay. "Let's just not panic," he said.

"I know we're so close, but it's too dark to go on," said Ollie. "I just wish we could go back home." His voice began to break, and Buck patted his friend's little shoulder. Together they held to each other, closing their eyes, trying not to cry. It was just as dark with their eyes closed or open now, yet their helpless situation seemed to magnify even more the surrounding night.

Buck heard Ollie whisper, "Heaven above, please help us. We're just two foolish squirrels lost here in the darkness."

Buck patted Ollie's shoulder again. Ollie opened his eyes a bit and to his great surprise, through his tears, he could somehow see light. Wiping his tears away, he could now see the whole forest around him.

"Buck," he said, "open your eyes!"

Buck opened his eyes and looked all around. Ollie began laughing at the expression of amazement on his friend's face. It was clear that Buck, too, could now see.

"It's the moon," cried Buck, "the silvery, full moon." And indeed, like a lantern showing them the way, the moon had come from behind a cloud, illuminating the snow-covered earth as bright as day. They could hardly believe it.

"I found the trail!" Ollie joyfully shouted.

"I can see where we are now," said Buck. "The southern maple grove is not far, just over the next ridge!"

The moon provided plenty of light as they continued up the hill, following their friend's footprints. Just before reaching the top, Ollie cried, "Buck, I can smell Mrs. Mole's mint tea!"

They stopped, and not only could they smell the tea, but they could hear music, and singing, and laughter.

"To the top," Buck said, and they were off again. Stopping the sleigh-basket at the crest of the ridge, they peered down the other side, and now they could see it all. There was the bonfire and all their forest friends who had gathered for the good food and merriment. Everyone was there, and the festivities were just about to begin.

Buck and Ollie looked at each other and shouted, "We made it!"

Chapter 7

The Feast

Buck and Ollie could hardly believe it! The Winter Feast with all their friends waited just below. The problems and hardships they faced on their journey: the snow, getting lost, and even the dark of night, were all behind them and didn't seem to matter now as the promise of a joyous reunion filled their thoughts.

"Let's ride the sleigh-basket down," suggested Ollie. And just that fast they climbed up on the pinecones, and away they went.

"Try to miss the bonfire," Buck shouted with a laugh.

"No problem, Buck," said Ollie, as they sped down the hill.

"Weeeeeeeee!" cried Ollie, and Buck joined in.

The forest animals looked up in amazement then together cheered as the sleigh-basket with Buck and Ollie came to a halt in their midst.

"Happy Winter Feast!" cried Buck and Ollie.

"Happy Winter Feast!" came a chorus of merry voices in reply, as all their friends gathered around.

"Buck and Ollie, it's so good to see you, but you had us worried," chided Mrs. Mole in her gentlest voice. "We've been wondering all day where you two were."

Ollie jumped down from the sleigh, and with the most excited expression imaginable, said, "Dear friends, may I say that it is so good for us to be home and to see you all again. Please forgive us for any worry we may have caused you. Buck and I have been on a long and dangerous journey, most secret in nature."

"Oh," came a wide-eyed response as the forest animals all looked at each other then turned again to fix their attention on Ollie.

He continued, "We've just this moment returned with the hope that you will be pleased with our presents."

"Of course, we're pleased to have you present with us," said Mr. Bear. "We're always honored by your presence," and everyone agreed.

Buck thought to himself, "How could they always be honored by our presents when we've never before given presents?" It bothered him just enough that he began looking around, and there, ironically, on a tree right beside him, he found what he was looking for.

It was another of the birch bark public notices like the one on Ollie's tree. He was hoping it might clear things up in his mind. "Winter Feast," it read, and as he continued, he paused on the words, "Your presence is requested…" He thought to himself, "Presents? Presence? Presence!" And just then, like biting into a bad nut, he realized he and Ollie had made a great mistake. The birch bark public notice requested their presence, not their presents! They weren't expected to bring presents; they were just supposed to be there, to be present. "No!" Buck thought. "Oh, my goodness, no!"

Jumping down beside his friend, he tapped Ollie on the shoulder and whispered, "Ollie, about the pinecones..."

He was about to explain to Ollie their huge blunder, but Ollie stopped him. "Oh of course, Buck," he said, "but please let me announce it. I've been working on a speech."

"A speech," said everyone.

"Well, let's hear it then, lad," said O'Possum, and everyone cheered.

Before Buck could stop him, Ollie cleared his throat and began. "Friend, there is nothing Buck and I enjoy more than the annual Winter Feast."

"Me too," said Mr. Bear.

"Shhhh," said Mrs. Rabbit. "you shouldn't interrupt a speech." Turning again to Ollie, with an apologetic look, she said, "Please continue."

"Uh, let's see," Ollie said. Once again, clearing his throat he continued. "When Buck and I read the birch bark public notice saying our presents were requested at the Winter Feast, we didn't know what to do. We couldn't think of a good present to give to such a fine group of friends."

Several eyebrows went up, and Ollie continued. "Don't worry, though, for we've just returned from beyond the tall pine forest with presents for everyone. Buck and I have them with us, right here in this sleigh-basket."

With the mention of presents, everyone looked at each other then cheered.

"It was nothing, my friend," Ollie said with a modest laugh. "And now, if Buck will assist me, we'll begin dispensing the gifts."

Before Buck could stop him, Ollie reached up and took down the first snow-covered pinecone. "Help me, Buck," he said.

Buck, not knowing what else to do, jumped back up on top of the sleigh-basket and started tossing down pinecones. Ollie began stacking them in a neat pile beside the bonfire

As they continued unloading the sleigh-basket, some of the forest animals began whispering to each other and giggling. They, too, realized Buck and Ollie had misunderstood the birch bark public notice.

"Their mistake has brought us good fortune," whispered O'Possum.

"Yes," said Woodpecker, "I wondered what the gift could be."

"It must be under those pinecones they're taking out of the basket," offered Mrs. Mole.

55

"In that case, then it must be a frightfully small gift as they are just about to the bottom of the basket," chuckled Mrs. Rabbit.

Buck had indeed reached the bottom of the basket. He reluctantly tossed the last pinecone down to Ollie, who caught it in his little paws. Ollie looked up at Buck, and with a look of total delight whispered excitedly, "Aren't you glad we didn't give up, Buck? Just look how happy we've made everyone."

Buck was looking, and he had been listening, too, as the other forest animals snickered and chuckled in hushed tones. He knew their giggling wasn't because they were happy, but rather because of the obvious mistake he and Ollie had made.

"What a pair of buffoons we've been," he thought, and as bad as Buck felt at that moment, he knew the worst was still to come. "After this is all over," he thought, "we'll be lucky if they don't stuff us and use us for bookends." His mind raced as fast as a squirrel's mind can, and yet there was nothing he could do or say to help ease this impending and awkward situation. It was too late, and now everyone was waiting for his gift.

"Friends," said Ollie. "All Buck and I want to say is HAPPY WINTER FEAST!" And with that he began handing out the pinecones.

First, he gave one each to Mrs. Rabbit and Mrs. Mole. "Well, thank you Ollie," they said, but they really didn't know what to say.

Next came Woodpecker and Mr. Bear. "Uh, thanks, Ollie. Uh, Buck, Uh, thank you," said Mr. Bear. And at least he did thank Buck and Ollie. Woodpecker, with beak wide open just kept looking back and forth between the pinecone, and Buck and Ollie.

Finally, O'Possum received his pinecone, and grinning as only O'Possum could, he said, "Thank you lad. I appreciate it."

Buck was hoping things would end there in polite silence, and indeed they would have except Mr. Bear was always one to get tickled easily. To this point he had restrained himself, but the sight of O'Possum's ridiculous grin triggered first a giggle, then a chuckle and then a full-blown bear laugh. Often laughter is contagious, and unfortunately this time it proved to be so, for soon almost all the forest animals had joined Mr. Bear in uncontrollable laughter.

Ollie turned to Buck and exclaimed, "Look how happy our gifts have made everyone."

Buck was so embarrassed, and as often happens when one is embarrassed, he was becoming quite angry inside.

Mrs. Mole tried to quiet everyone, but her shushing only seemed to make things worse.

"A dangerous journey," laughed Mr. Bear as he rolled about in the snow.

"Hope you are pleased with our presents," giggled Woodpecker.

"It was nothing, my friends," hooted O'Possum. "HAPPY WINTER FEAST!" And again, they broke into a new round of hysterics.

Ollie's expression was changing from sheer joy to confusion. "They do like our presents, don't they Buck?" he asked.

Buck answered Ollie by looking back at the others and shouting, "Don't you see, Ollie? They're laughing at us."

With this, the unkind laughter did cease, but the silence that followed was even more unpleasant. Ollie looked into the eyes of his forest neighbors and asked, "Is this true; you are laughing at us?"

"We're not laughing at you," explained Mr. Bear. "We're just sort of laughing at your gift."

"When you insult a gift, you insult the giver of the gift as well," replied Buck.

"But lad," said O'Possum, holding up his pinecone, "You have given something that is common, and you call it a gift?"

"If this gift is so common," Buck said, "then just throw it away."

With that, Buck picked up one of the remaining pinecones and heaved it into the bonfire. "Just throw it away!" he cried.

Ollie stood there in silent disbelief. The present Big Apple Tree had promised would be such a wonderful surprise, and that he and Buck had labored so hard to bring back, was now burning before their eyes

Chapter 8

The Gift

The forest animals stood there in silence with their heads hanging in shame. The only sound to be heard was the crackling of the fire where Buck had just thrown the pinecone.

"Maybe these silly pinecones didn't seem like such a great gift," said Buck, "but what you couldn't see was how they were filled with Ollie's love for you."

Buck turned to his little grey companion and said, "I'm so sorry, Ollie."

Ollie just stood there staring at the flames. Suddenly he pointed and exclaimed, "Buck, look what's happening to the fire!"

Buck turned and together they watched as the most wonderful sight filled their eyes. The pinecone was indeed burning, but never had there been a more beautiful flame. Mixed in among the familiar yellow flickers and moving together as in a festive dance, were a variety of hues each seemingly more breathtaking than the previous.

The rest of the forest animals drew near as the fire continued to blaze in the most amazing colors imaginable; blues, greens, reds, oranges and yellow, and combinations of all. There came a chorus of, "Ooooohs," as everyone now watched in delightful surprise.

Mrs. Rabbit looked at her pinecone, and turning to O'Possum said, "Perhaps they only look common."

Now she, too, tossed her pinecone into the fire and again the beautiful colors brought a pleasant ovation of, "ooooohs" and "aaaahhhs."

"Buck and Ollie, I am so sorry I laughed at your gift," she said, sincerely. "Please forgive me."

Before Buck or Ollie could respond, Mrs. Mole said, "Yes, I believe we all need to apologize for our unspeakable behavior."

"I believe I speak for everyone," said O'Possum, with hat in hand, "when I say I feel just beastly about our lack of gratitude in response to your benevolence."

Everyone agreed, including Mr. Bear, who was not at all familiar with the word benevolence, but who did wish to extend his apology. "Could you ever find it in your hearts, Buck and Ollie, to forgive us for laughing at you and your wonderful gift?" he asked.

One thing about squirrels, they are quick to forgive and forget. "No harm done," said Ollie.

"Don't mention it," added Buck. "Let's just enjoy this time together as true friends should," and from everyone, a loud hooray followed.

They were all hugging and laughing now, and one by one each began tossing their pinecone into the fire. Woodpecker struck up a festive tune on his accordion. The merry sounds of, "Ooooohs and "Aaaahhhs," laughter and hands clapping together in time to the music resounded higher and higher as each pinecone seemed to burn more beautifully than the last.

O'Possum tossed his pinecone into the fire, then turning to Mrs. Rabbit, he bowed. Laughing, she took his hand, and together, arm in arm, they skipped around the bonfire. Woodpecker's accordion played as everyone clapped and cheered.

"Buck," said Mrs. Mole, "could you assist me with my pinecone? I'm afraid I am a bit too small."

"Certainly," said Buck, and he tossed it into the fire.

Mr. Bear said, "I guess that's the last one," and a final chorus of, "Ooooohs" and "Aaaahhhs" broke out. This time, however, their "Ooooohs" were joined by another "Ooooo," coming from a tree limb high above the bonfire.

Everyone looked up, and to their great, gasping surprise they saw none other than the wise Mr. Owl. It took their breath away just to look upon his noble stately appearance. Woodpecker, in fact, proving untrue to his own words, took one look at the majestic Mr. Owl, and straight away fainted beak first into a snowbank. His accordion sounded as the bellows blared a confused mixture of notes into a dissonant strain. Mr. Bear and O'Possum helped him up, brushing the snow from his face. He was fine, of course, except for the embarrassment of it all.

Mrs. Rabbit, wishing to draw the attention away from Woodpecker and his awkwardness, said, "Welcome, Mr. Owl. It is such a delight to have you visit our humble little forest." She bowed gracefully, and as if following her cue, everyone else bowed. You could tell by some of the clumsier bowing going on that most were not accustomed to such formality.

"Thank you, Mrs. Rabbit," began Mr. Owl. His voice was so kind and distinctive. "Friends," he said, "I've been meaning to visit you for some time, and your Winter Feast has afforded me this opportunity both to visit, and of course, to sample Mrs. Rabbit's world-famous carrot cake. It would be a shame to miss out on that."

Everyone agreed with a chuckle, and Mrs. Rabbit smiled a blushing smile.

Woodpecker, with traces of snow still visible on his beak, had recovered sufficiently from his fainting spell to brave a welcome of his own. "We are all so honored by your presence," he said.

Mr. Owl nodded, and with a kind smile said, "I see your two lively grey squirrel neighbors have also honored you with their, uh, presents," and everyone laughed a loving laugh.

As Ollie listened it kept running through his head that somehow, he knew Mr. Owl, and yet he knew they had never met. Suddenly it came to him. What was familiar to Ollie was Mr. Owl's voice. It was the same voice he and Buck had heard coming from Big Apple Tree. "Buck," he whispered.

"I know," Buck whispered back, for he, too, had recognized the voice.

Mr. Owl spoke, "Well done, Buck and Ollie. Your pinecones were truly a remarkable gift, and yet, at first, not received as gifts at all. Seen as common and thought to be ordinary, they were laughed at and discarded. It was only then that we came to, shall we say, see the light of just how truly magical and wondrous they were.

But friends, more than pinecones, Buck and Ollie's gift to you was their love. There can be no greater gift, and love comes to us in many forms. Consider the beauty of the earth and the heavens above. Are these not gifts from our creator showing his great love for us? If we listen, we can hear His love in the song of baby robins in springtime and the whispers of a summertime breeze blowing through a field of purple wildflowers? Can we not see His love when autumn leaves are transformed before our very eyes into their spectacular fiery brilliance? Yes, even with a quiet, gentle winter's snowfall we can see our creator's love for His creation.

To some, these are looked upon as everyday and common. I choose to see them as miracles and gifts most precious."

Smiling, Mr. Owl continued. "As my gift, let me share with you a story to warm your hearts on this cold winter's night."

The forest animals applauded, then at Mr. Owl's direction, they sat down around the bonfire. Gazing upward, they eagerly awaited his story.

Mr. Owl began. "Once there was a star, a spectacular star, here for a season, and now gone. Some say that dust from this magical star fell to earth not far from here in a valley just beyond the tall pine forest. Who can say?"

He shifted to one side, and as he did, there, in one of his great talons, a snow-covered pinecone could be seen.

"The one we left in the tree," whispered Ollie, and Buck, without turning, nodded his agreement.

Mr. Owl continued. "What I can tell you of the star is that it was sent to guide us to Heaven's greatest gift. No, it wasn't gold, silver, precious stones or gems, nothing so common as those. The gift of which I speak was, of all things, a tiny baby, a boy child born to mankind. But more than a baby, He was the long ago promised King.

The birth of a King announced by a star, you would expect to find him in a warm palace, knowing only the finest of comforts. Yes, and yet, that was not the way it happened. This gift, this child was born, in of all places, a stable, a barn with animals all around.

There were no fine wrappings, in fact His bed was nothing more than a trough, filled with hay. I'm afraid at first he didn't look like much of a gift at all. But for those with eyes to see, and hearts to believe, in this child was wrapped the very gift of Heaven's love.

Nobles and shepherds alike knelt before Him, and Heaven overflowed with angels singing, 'Joy to the world, peace and goodwill to all,' for the King is born. And His rule would be that of love and kindness, even calling us His friends. and commanding us to love one another. And so," Mr. Owl continued, "In this cold, dark, wonderful season of winter, let us remember that as Heaven so loved the world, we are to love one another."

He then released his pinecone, letting it drop into the fire, and with all eyes on the flame, he said, "May Heaven's love ever be found in us. Let it be as a fire warming our hearts and a light guiding our path." Then spreading his great wings, he exclaimed, "My friends, I wish you peace and joy. Happy Winter Feast!"

All the forest animals stood to their feet with cheers and applause, and even the fire seemed to blaze up as in approval. Mr. Owl glided downward, landing gracefully in their midst.

"Thank you," Woodpecker said, bowing to Mr. Owl. "Your story has brought to us all, great and small, such wonderful good tidings," and everyone agreed.

Then, with hands joining in a circle around the bonfire, they sang a song of thanksgiving for all their blessings. Afterward they enjoyed the feast with its bountiful good food, mint tea and fellowship.

As the music played and festivities continued, Ollie again had his list out and was marking through the last items. Buck leaned closer to see what was being scratched out. It read 'Gifts given,' and 'Enjoy the Winter Feast'.

"I'm glad you were able to mark those last two items off your list," Buck said with a laugh.

"Me too," said Ollie. "It's been quite an adventure, hasn't it?"

"More like a dream," Buck replied. "Everything was so magical, the snow, the pinecones...."

"Mr. Owl's presence," they recited in unison, followed with another laugh.

"I'll never forget it," Ollie marveled aloud, "and though I'm sure I'll never understand everything, wasn't this the best Winter Feast ever?"

"The best 'til next year," promised Buck with a laugh.

And every winter since, the gentle creatures of Hickory Mountain have gathered together with joyful peace and goodwill to celebrate the Winter Feast.

The End

About the Author/Illustrator

Brian Kinder was born and raised in Fredericktown Missouri. He served eight years in the Air Force, then settled in Little Rock, receiving a BA and MA in Music Education and Visual Arts from University of Arkansas, Little Rock. For twenty plus years, Brian taught Music and Art in Little Rock schools. He is best known, however, as a singer/songwriter of original children's music. Along with his wife, Terri, the Kinders have released twelve award winning audio CD's and annually perform hundreds of kid's concerts in Arkansas and surrounding states. This is Brian's first book.